this OR that?
weather

winter storm

OR

blizzard?

Kelly Doudna

Consulting Editor, Diane Craig, M.A./Reading Specialist

Super Sandcastle

An Imprint of Abdo Publishing
abdopublishing.com

abdopublishing.com

Published by Abdo Publishing, a division of ABDO, PO Box 398166, Minneapolis, Minnesota 55439. Copyright © 2016 by Abdo Consulting Group, Inc. International copyrights reserved in all countries. No part of this book may be reproduced in any form without written permission from the publisher. Super SandCastle™ is a trademark and logo of Abdo Publishing.

Printed in the United States of America, North Mankato, Minnesota
102015
012016

THIS BOOK CONTAINS
RECYCLED MATERIALS

Editor: Liz Salzmann
Content Developer: Nancy Tuminelly
Cover and Interior Design and Production: Mighty Media, Inc.
Photo Credits: Kelly Doudna, NASA, NOAA, Shutterstock

Library of Congress Cataloging-in-Publication Data
Doudna, Kelly, 1963- author.
  Winter storm or blizzard? / Kelly Doudna ; consulting editor, Diane Craig.
    pages cm -- (This or that? Weather)
  ISBN 978-1-62403-958-4
1. Blizzards--Juvenile literature. I. Craig, Diane, editor. II. Title.
  QC926.37.D65 2016
  551.55'5--dc23
                 2015021247

Super SandCastle™ books are created by a team of professional educators, reading specialists, and content developers around five essential components—phonemic awareness, phonics, vocabulary, text comprehension, and fluency—to assist young readers as they develop reading skills and strategies and increase their general knowledge. All books are written, reviewed, and leveled for guided reading and early reading intervention programs for use in shared, guided, and independent reading and writing activities to support a balanced approach to literacy instruction.

contents

winter storm or blizzard?

Is it a winter storm? Or is it a blizzard? Do you know the difference?

A winter storm forms during cold weather. This usually happens in the winter. But a winter storm can also form in late fall or early spring.

A blizzard is a **severe** winter storm. It happens in the winter. It has high winds. Blowing snow makes it hard to see.

windy weather

A winter storm has snow. But it doesn't have strong winds.

A blizzard has very strong winds. The wind blows 35 miles per hour (56 kmh) or more. The wind lasts at least three hours.

let it snow!

A winter storm happens during cold weather. A winter storm makes snow, sleet, freezing rain, and ice. Sometimes there's even thundersnow!

A blizzard blows snow around. The snow usually falls during the storm. In a ground blizzard, the wind picks up snow from the ground.

how far can you see?

Snow from a winter storm can be
heavy. But it doesn't blow around.
You can still see through it.

A blizzard's winds blow snow around.
The snow **swirls**. It fills the air. That
makes it hard to see. In a blizzard you
can't see farther than ¼ mile (0.4 km).

meeting of the masses

A winter storm happens when cold air moves south. It runs into warmer air. The storm forms where the air masses meet.

A blizzard is more **extreme**. The difference between the cold and warm air masses is big. This makes the storm stronger. A blizzard happens on the northwest side of the storm.

isn't that special?

Lake-effect snow is a special kind of snowstorm. Cold air moves over a lake. The water is warmer than the air. Water vapor rises into the cold air. It freezes into heavy snow.

cold air

lots of snow

water vapor

warmer water

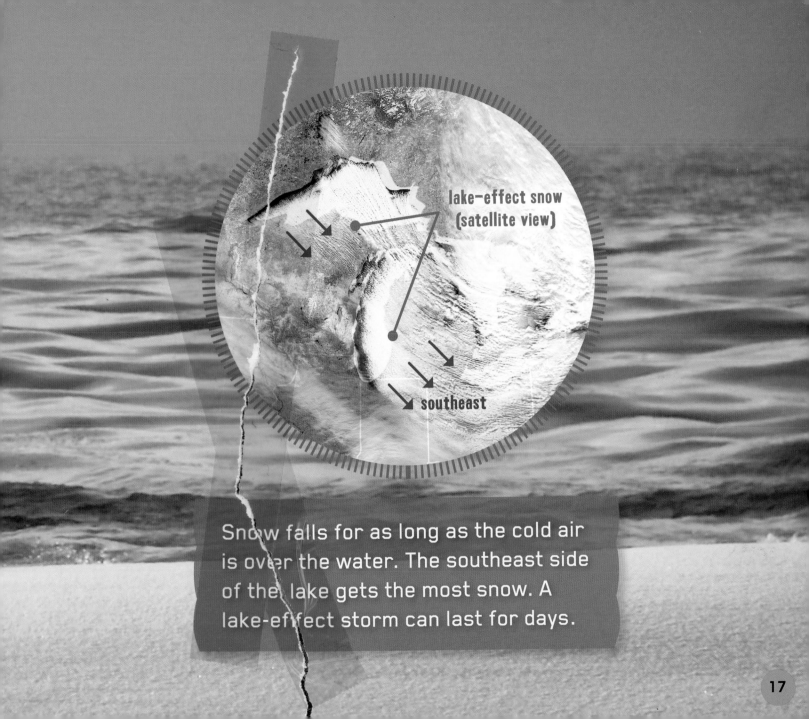

lake-effect snow
(satellite view)

southeast

Snow falls for as long as the cold air is over the water. The southeast side of the lake gets the most snow. A lake-effect storm can last for days.

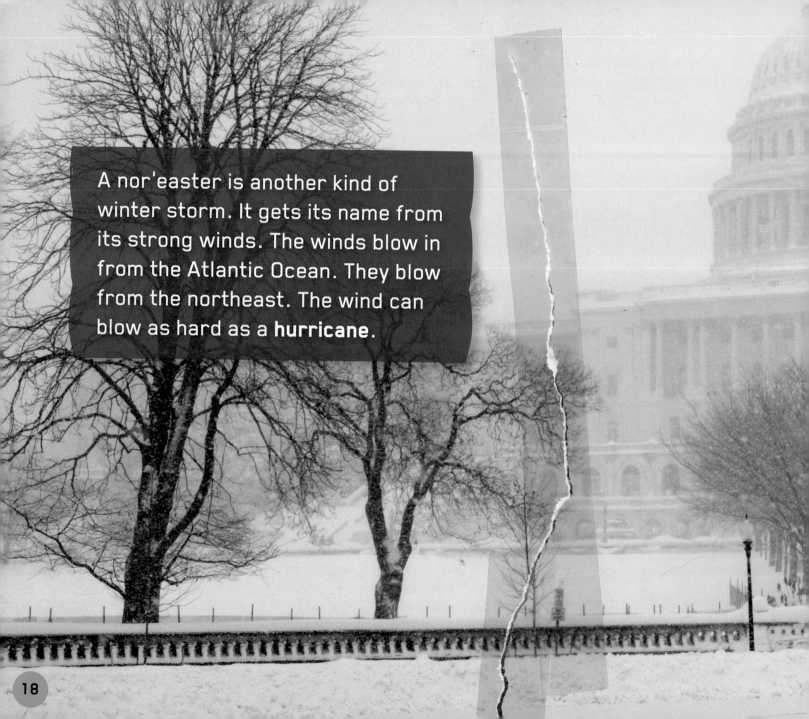

A nor'easter is another kind of winter storm. It gets its name from its strong winds. The winds blow in from the Atlantic Ocean. They blow from the northeast. The wind can blow as hard as a **hurricane**.

A nor'easter forms in the south. Then it moves up the east coast. It becomes very powerful. A nor'easter makes heavy snow. It makes big waves in the Atlantic Ocean.

take care!

A winter storm is **dangerous**. Ice makes the ground **slippery**. Walking and driving are hard. Buildings and trees get **damaged**.

A blizzard's cold wind is dangerous. It fills the air with snow. People can't see. It's easy to get lost in a blizzard.

✳ at a glance ✳

winter storm ——————— blizzard

created by cold and warm ——————— created by cold and warm
air masses meeting ——————— air masses meeting

can occur in fall, winter, or spring ——————— occurs in winter

may or may not have strong winds ——— winds stronger than 35 mph (56 kmh)

heavy snowfall ——————— blowing snow

danger from **slippery** areas ——— danger from wind and blowing snow

bunny in a blizzard

does glitter hide the critter?

What You'll Need
- jar with screw-on lid
- hot glue gun and glue sticks
- plastic critter
- glitter
- water

1 Take the lid off the jar. Glue the **critter** to the inside of the lid. Let the glue dry.

2 Put glitter in the jar. Make it about ½ inch (1.3 cm) deep.

3 Fill the jar with water.

4 Screw the lid on tightly. Turn the jar over.

5 **Swirl** the jar. Get the glitter moving!

6 Look into the jar. Can you see the critter through the glitter?

think about it

How is the glitter like snowflakes? How is the swirling water like wind?

glossary

critter – any animal.

damage – harm or ruin.

dangerous – able or likely to cause harm or injury.

extreme – very much, or to a very great degree.

hurricane – a tropical storm with very high winds that starts in the ocean and moves toward land.

severe – serious, extreme, intense, or dangerous.

slippery – having a smooth, wet, icy, or oily surface that is easy to slide on.

swirl – to whirl or to move smoothly in circles.